ART, UNIONS, ARTIFICIAL INTELLIGENCE AND MONEY

By

Anthony David Padgett

Published by
ADP Publishing

First Published 2020

Dedication

To All Artists

"We live in a dream when we define ourselves by our aspirations and not our situations." Anthony Padgett

INDEX

INTRODUCTION

1. THE CURRENT SITUATION

2. HISTORY

3. FINANCES

4. REGULATION

5. ARTIFICIAL INTELLIGENCE

6. WAYS FORWARD

INTRODUCTION

This essay is based on my 30 years' experience of rejections and successes as an artist and my short time with the Artists Union of England (including my training as a Union Representative). It is not indicative of the ideas of the AUE or its members. I would like to thank Theresa Easton and Pam Foley have given me a great amount of help with the AUE, however, I don't want people to think my ideas are representative of views and ideas that they or the AUE hold. Rather, it contains my own, personal perspective and ideas.

My joining the Artists Union of England arose out of my art projects "A Year With Picasso". Discovering that Picasso was active at the World Peace Congress in 1950 and also that he was a multi-millionaire member of the Communist party. It allowed me to reframe a key issue, the regulation of the art industry, in terms of being a worker. My method of creation of art has used a system of categorisation that is empirical and phenomenological and is almost computer like. The work that I make is original but hasn't been recognised. And it is my belief that Artificial Intelligence will bring about regulation in the art industry and also the creation of new artworks.

This essay will fundamentally change your way of thinking. You will no doubt disagree with much of it on a conscious level but the ideas will filter through to your unconscious mind and then later you may well have the idea, in a slightly different form or context, and think that you have originated it. This process would occur whether you read this introduction or not. But at least if you read it you might be conscious of the process and remember where you first came across the following ideas.

Such processes go on in the viewing and creation of art. And this is why registers of art are important - to do justice to the original creators of pieces of work. Artists don't always intend to steal from their fellow artists (though some are happy to do this and see it as normal behaviour). I believe that this reform is the most important for artists and that unions are the best placed to bring about his change to a corrupted art-world.

Art has become about money and is chosen by people who are unaccountable and unconnected to the tastes of ordinary people. It is influenced by a commercial world of buyers with their own personal tastes and who is, as Oscar Wilde wrote, "a man who knows the price of everything, and the value of nothing." And, as I say "art bought by people who don't understand what they are buying, sold by people who don't understand what they are selling and made by artists who don't understand what they are making." And the rest of us in society are then told we should believe it is art, whether we understand it or not.

Some believe this is how art has always been. And yet other work practices have evolved. So why not those for art? The current situation is that there is little or no transparency in the selection and promotion of art by institutions and commercial galleries. And this lack of transparency allows for theories to be created. The defence against these theories is that there is no evidence for them so they are just conspiracy theories. However, with the restriction of evidence by the people in power it is a Catch 22 situation. The only way out of this is to posit theories and propose future solutions. Artificial Intelligence provides the hope of a possible solution – provided artists can unite to call for its positive use before it gets controlled by the institutions to reinforce their power structures.

As artists - united we are valued, divided we are ignored. Anthony Padgett 2020

1. THE CURRENT SITUATION

THE LACK OF DEFINITIONS OF ART

The terms Art and Artist are so vague that they are almost impossible to define. And any definition will find artists who try to break beyond that definition. Art is notoriously difficult to define. In the 1953 "Philosophical Investigations" of Ludwig Wittgenstein he showed how even a notion like a "game" eluded a clear definition. Two things we can take from this are that there is nothing unique in our failing to define the term "art", and that even if impossible to define a simple term we can still create working definitions and that allows movement between uncertainties. Philosophically, we cannot rationally prove that a world exists outside our own consciousness, but empirically we still choose to function as if it does. And it is the same with art. We can create working definitions. It is not the purpose of this essay to look for an exact definition of art. However, so that the reader knows my perspective, my working definition is: a creative, original or aesthetic formal expression through a medium and/or as the medium itself. To really generalise I would define art as "an expression."

"Artist" is a historical term that has changed over time. It has become more inclusive as what constitutes art has become broader. Access to training to be an artist has become wider. And this has allowed for the removal of discrimination and prejudice over who (race, gender etc) can be an artist. Unfortunately a new discrimination has entered over who is a "good" or "successful" artist. And this is based on sales and how much money an artist makes. However, good judgement has also been removed, and this allows discrimination and prejudice to remain unchallenged.

Lack of definition allows for multiple injustices to occur. Even if a definition isn't possible galleries and curators should still provide a rationale for their choices to be transparent, sanctioned and not just subjective. Without this the intent and purpose of art is hidden. It has become a rich person's game, monopolised by the wealthy. In this game only "paid" for art has value. Economically poorer people (namely the poorer artists) should reclaim art from this limited view. But for this to happen a more universal definition or understanding of art is required so that poorer peoples' art cannot be devalued by the rich.

FORM VS CONTENT - ART VS PROPAGANDA

The next issue is how to define the "expression" as good or not. There is an antinomy between art that is purely formal (the style of the lines, colours, shapes etc) and art that has content (subject, stories, themes etc). The purely formal can become formulaic and the artist's life can be the subject of interest for the art lover. Alternatively the interesting subject matter can become all that is of interest.

Art used to show ideas and ideology through its narrative scenes. Because art became formal the art selectors ensured artists complied with the art ideologies. You can see this in how in the 1950s the US government favoured the work of Jackson Pollock (an American individualist) as opposed to the social realists (whose work depicted workers in idealised scenes) of the Communist government. On the one side is social realism (figurative and moralising) and on the other is pure abstraction (non-representational and formal qualities).

After the Abstract expressionists, the Pop Artists created figurative art in semi-ironic comment on the advertising images of American corporations. This had a resemblance to the narrative content of soviet propaganda only it was an idealisation of consumer life (instead of worker life).

For me, there is a tension between Unions as political Left Wing and artists as making non-political expressions, free of doctrines. Supporting political parties and ethical issues was a key concern of the unions and members had to automatically pay to support the Labour Party until this was outlawed (with contributions now becoming voluntary following the Trade Union and Labour Relations (Consolidation) Act 1992).

Unions want issue based art. This is propaganda and is not necessary in union art. Similarly the act of abstraction was seen as political and spiritual in the early communist work of Kandinsky and Malevich etc. This creative activity was appropriated into capitalist structures and stripped of its political message. And the communist countries found favour with social realism because they became self-aggrandising in a worker / leader narrative art. Similarly Adolf Hitler saw modern art as degenerate because it broke down the Social Realist ideals that he aspired towards for the German race.

Fine Art could be seen as academic. And applied art as issue based. However, because the ruling elite keep control of what constitutes Fine Art they also keep control the issues in Applied Art and can make sure they only allow the ones that they want to have shown.

For me the content is secondary to the form. It is art because of the form. The content of a piece of art should neither support nor prejudice whether the art is good as art in a formal sense. A message can be added in which case the art is applied to the message. Some propaganda may stand out as memorable applied art. To the general public this might be a key reason why it is seen as art.

Propaganda can also be seen as illustration, advertising. And when art becomes a copy of other art it is a form of advertising the pre-existing art.

Art is about value. And what that value is depends from person to person. Art can have its own value or be about an agenda, a propaganda. People for whom commerce is the most important value are buying art and saying this is what art is about. If artists allow art's value to be based in specific subjects and themes then it is easier for them to be controlled by the purchaser, the buyer who can decide what themes and subjects they think are important and art.

An empirical analysis of the elements of an artwork is possible and this gives discourse of forms of art and not content. Content is an infinite subject matter that can hide bias as selection becomes based on the subject matter that strikes a resonance and this resonance is based on discriminatory criteria. Counter-intuitively, by making art that is based on political issues it allows for unfair political issues to continue to be represented. Rather than by basing work on its formal quality.

There is therefore a moral and political dimension in the content of art, but there is also a moral and political dimension in the form of art, or rather the way in which opportunities are given and the form is assessed and valued. If only certain groups have access to opportunities to create quality work then they are kept excluded – hence equity is about affording people equality of opportunity. But without regulation and feedback levels of equality and equity cannot be established.

Art should not be primarily a tool for propaganda or advertising. If it is just a tool then its true nature and beauty can never be explored and valued. It is an end in itself. And that end can by its very nature is political. It is rational and valuing the creativity of all and any person regardless of race, creed, sex, sexuality, disability, age and religion. Hence if an artist has an original voice then they can work around moral issues and it still be original art. An example of this is Picasso's using his sharp, angular Cubist style to paint "Guernica" in 1936, whose subject matter was the bombing of civilians by the Nazis in support of Franco's fascist revolt in Spain. But if the voice is drowned by the moral issues then the arts real political value (of being able to create cultural work that brakes from cultural servitude) is overlooked. Its real political value is the fair assessment of the value and worth of art. The structure of art making in its self is a union based activity if within a register to fairly assess artists' work.

Artists are usually Product Led in a society that values Market Led. Market led is what people want to buy and product led is what you want people to buy. The advertising helps persuade people that your product is what they want to buy.

Similarly the subject matter can help persuade people that your product is art, and that Art is what the Market needs. Advertising has been used to promote art and set the cultural agenda. Dealers like advertiser Charles Saatchi were known for the promotion of artists' work. In 2004 the exhibition and temporary loan of Saatchi's £200 million collection (including Damien Hirst's work) to the Tate Galleries was opposed by Serota but he gave in to Damien Hirst's donation, in 2007, of Hirst's own work as Saatchi had no effective, objective frame to justify the decision that Hirst's financially significant work hadn't become significant art. Saatchi's promotion, based on subjectivity and the power of money, had won over through, Hirst, one of his art superstars.

OBJECTIVITY AND SUBJECTIVITY

Ironically, the current received wisdom that "Art is subjective" is spoken by people as if it were an objective statement. Yet the statement "Art is objective" is treated like a subjective error.

There is an antinomy (an irreconcilable opposition and interrelation) between objectivity and subjectivity in judgment. All objectivity has a subjective element, and all subjectivity has an objective element. It is impossible to describe subjective experience without objective ideas. And it is impossible to describe a subjective response to art without objective categories and terms. However, it has become fashionable to say that art is just subjective and that it cannot be objectively categorised. This is a form of scepticism similar to believing everything is within your mind and that there is no objective reality. Scepticism about an external world cannot be disproved by rational argument but common sense prevails that there is a real world. Analysis of art is more complex and so allows people to maintain scepticism say that it is all subjective. A lesser form of scepticism is to say that we cannot view facts about art separately from our emotional responses to it. There is a sliding scale and whilst inseparable in the final analysis it is useful to make a largely empirical analysis that excludes the emotional content.

Formal analysis of art had been focussed around abstract art in the 1950s and 1960s. Postmodern Art (about Performance and the human body) was opposed to the categorisation and classification of abstract Formalism. The fashion for subjectivity in art comes from a social and political post-modern rejection of the abstract formalism in the 1960s but now, enough work has been created that a formal analysis of narrative and theme based post-modernism can be made. This is not to look at the content, just the way that the content is expressed.

In the twentieth century the Postmodern perspective removed the focus from formal standards and in its place put social expressions, narratives and stories.

Some confusion about Postmodernism occurs as it also refers to a 1980s period of irony and lack of belief in any values. This contrasts with the earnest political campaigning of the 1960s. What unites both is that they present issues of narrative rather than purely formal concerns. To coincide with Postmodern Political art Pop art took off because popular culture (films, comics etc.) had become the general public's source of aesthetic satisfaction. Abstract art wasn't accessible to the general buyer, so comics, films and celebrities etc. became art. People didn't want the uncomfortable, social and political issues of Postmodernism interfering with their aesthetic enjoyment. And in the 1990s Charles Saatchi's agenda in advertising art was to promote his hero artists using "shock" to entertain, or titillate, rather than genuinely challenge, his audiences, e.g. Hirst's Shark in formaldehyde and Emin's unmade bed. This was to improve their value within a Thatcherite and Neo Liberal agenda.

When art is about Form it is easier to be objective in its assessment e.g. many contemporary pieces may look highly original very similar works have been done – e.g. Damien Hirst's "The Physical Impossibility of Death in the Mind of Someone Living" 1991 Shark in a glass tank has similarities to Jeff Koon's earlier "One Ball Total Equilibrium Tank" 1985 basketball in a glass tank. Or Tracey Emin's "My Bed" 1998 installation of an unmade bed has similarities to Louise Bourgoise's earlier installation of a made bed in "Red Room Parents" 1994. When it is about Content, Themes and Values then it is more subjective and claims of originality can hide in statements of what the work is "about" It also can directly appeal to whether the viewer agrees with those themes and issues, or if they are about the viewer's life and reinforce their experiences and prejudices.

Subjectivity still comes into choices regarding the realms of quality of a piece of work. Standards to say why work is selected and then this can be contested. Art criticism has become about rhetoric with quality assumed and not analysed. But by whose subjectivity is this rhetoric designed to appeal to. We need to return to Formal standards if we are to get justification of decisions. Appeals to "subjectivity" allow the art chooser to say that they have a special aesthetic sensitivity and ability to find an artist.

ART HERO VS ART COLLECTIVE

There is also an antinomy between Art Hero/Heroine and Design/Art Collective that is part of the structure of human thinking. The vision of the artist as hero, like Odysseus tied to the mast of the ship facing madness, is almost needed to make progress in art and find new creative directions. Then the art industry provides workers to create the outcomes of the trouble-shooting. Perhaps another maverick taking the findings of Odysseus and perfecting them. However, this model is a myth, a Fairy tale.

A small number of hero artists make a living from art, yet without all the other competing artists the small number wouldn't exist and there would be no artistic development. And you will never get rid of a sense of community from artists. Conversely, you will never get rid of a sense of egotistical capitalist competition either. Currently the balance has gone too far in favour of egotistical capitalist competition. I am not against competition. I am against unfair competition.

Ideas of the artist hero have been reinforced by ideas of the corporate hero who has not built a family business by hard work, rather "the Reagan business hero was the corporate take-over artist. Any regulations that might get in the way of these ruthless new capitalists were removed" (1). And whilst, with the Industrial Revolution, we have moved politically from aristocracy to democracy - economically we still behave like aristocracies, or have returned to behaving like aristocracies (2). The US is controlled by 400 billionaires. And not only are these economic aristocracies undermining our democracies, they are also undermining the academic basis of our art (3).

Against this hero notion is the idea of the art collective. Here is where the union come in. However
Artists don't want Trade Unions because they want to be famous. Many artists are hypocrites thinking that they are collaborative but they are really out for themselves. Some are openly out for themselves and aware of this. Art has become a competition with winners and losers positioning themselves in a hierarchy. For some an artist's goal is to sell work and be famous. They don't want shared glory. They want exclusive stardom. For those people, perhaps the union of artists can be in a system where if there is a public issue then the artist whose work fits the issue can becomes the hero for that moment. They are famous for 15 minutes (aka Warhol) but are still part of the real hero, the Art Union. For others, myself included, art is a vocation, a calling or instinct to create and be engaged in aesthetics. Although I would be happy with a substantial degree of recognition for my work. And an important distinction should be drawn between a modest motivation of recognition and a more egotistical motivation of fame. From recognition it is hoped that financial reward will follow. This occurs only for a very few people and fame is required for a reasonable financial reward. This produces confusion as recognition should be enough to provide a reasonable reward. However, because art has "heroes" we find just the top percentage making conspicuous amounts of money.

The galleries (with their critics and curators) choose to write some artists "in" and other artists "out" of history. These galleries and their artists will be out of history unless they opt for inclusivity as their artists may be found to be lacking. The union is an alternative goal and can be achieved primarily through a systematic artistic register and secondarily through academic credibility. People need stories and hero figures. But the union is about collective histories and so the new hero is the union.

So we need to educate at college and school level to change explanations and the naïve view of art history. We need to undermine the myths of the individual hero artists, to show how their work arose out of contexts of other artists, and prevent the artist from being located in the single object and show, instead, the history of how they got to that work.

2. SOME HISTORY

TRADE UNIONS AND ART PROFESSIONAL BODIES

The Fine arts of oil painting on canvas and sculpting in stone and bronze came out of earlier crafts and trades using ceramics and simple forms. In the Twentieth century artists rediscovered old materials and skills and created new materials and skills. And so art became more closely associated to materials and methods of other, even prehistoric, ages. So should art return to being seen as a trade?

The history of art is related to history of the patrons and supporters of art. Patrons included aristocrats, merchants and the church. And art was part of religious cultural expression. Now, without religion as dominant, we find art has a broader cultural as well as commercial role. Historically art was a trade/craft but it became the leisure activity of the wealthy and a vocation for the elite – but it was promoted as applying worth over all artists, including the proletariat. Saying the elite make better work than the poorer artists because it is in the elites institutions, selected by the elite. The elite displaced the high end craftsmen with their own artist "factory owners" e.g. Andy Warhol, Damien Hirst and Antony Gormley, who then employ the craftsmen to make their own works.

The working structures that produced the master craftsmen have been removed and replaced with elite, fee paying institutions that require no great training to enter. Access becomes based on knowledge, where and to whom you were born and who you know - rather than on skill. And, rather than sharing finances and status amongst artists of equal merit, they reject the mass of the poorer artists (whilst including some as tokenism to justify their position). To spread appreciation across a broader range of artists then we might need to turn art back into being seen as a trade.

London Art is connected with the ruling London Elite. The Industrial revolution brought power to Employers from the North and the Midlands in the nineteenth and twentieth centuries. This revolution was, to an extent, meritocratic and based on skills. This meritocracy had some effect in the arts, however, the London based Elite have slowly re-asserted their power and devalued the industries and industrialists as well as the unions of the workers in those industries. Instead, they preferred the South based financial and professional (especially legal) sectors. And the arts and media are now dominated by these wealthy figures.

John Ruskin and William Morris were two of the progenitors of the idea of "Guild Socialism" and of "National Guilds", in which craftsmen would come into their own again. The objective of Guild Socialism was also workers' control of industry – but attained by evolutionary, not revolutionary, means. This take-over of an industry by the workers within it is called "Syndicalism" (4). A craft guild like this is a forerunner to an Artists- Union. And the Royal Academy in London seems to be like this, only it is an elite, exclusive workers Syndicalism. "On a winter's day in 1768, architect Sir William Chambers visited the king, George III. He brought with him a petition signed by 36 artists and architects including himself, all of whom were seeking permission to "establish a society for promoting the Arts of Design". What's more, they also proposed an annual exhibition and a School of Design." (5)

One of the Union of Post Office Workers' declared objectives was: "the organisation of Post Office Workers into a comprehensive industrial union with a view to the Service being ultimately conducted and managed by the Guild." This was a form of Syndicalism. The Guilds (like the Royal Academy) protected against competition. (6) These guilds faded in front of new markets. Art kept its old, pre-industrial work mode. Currently the majority of artists are losing income in an industrial art economy. And this is not just in relation to reproductions and the moving image but due to their not being fairly assessed and in terms of who is judged to be a proper artist. Now is the time for an Industrial Revolution in the Art Industry.

In the 18th century (when the Royal Academy was formed) ordinary workers discussing the pay and conditions at work was illegal under the Combination Act. This meant that Collective Bargaining (where workers discuss their pay and come to an agreement on how they want to discuss that with their employer) was illegal. Workers had to accept what they were given but Journeymen still formed combinations to calculate just demands. But combinations were tolerated if there was no trouble. Then, in 1799, William Pitt (PM) made punishment severe and allowed for workers to be laid off easily and en masse. (7)

In the 1830s the Tolpuddle Martyrs were exiled as criminals for meeting to people who discussed wage levels. This was less than the Royal Academy were doing. No Kings protectionism there even though the Royal Academy is like a Trade Union in that it is an organisation about workers that regulates relations with employers on collective issues. And if an organisation does this then it is considered to be a trade union that then has a subject to statutory requirements of submitting annual reports. (8) Collective Bargaining between a Union Representative and Employer (where the Union power is recognised) was a way to get a fairer deal for employees. But this can lead to rising prices. If wage levels increase then the cost to make the goods increases. This is why, historically, parliament thought that it had the right to set wages (and ensure the pound followed the gold standard) and why it was sedition for workers to organise for pay rises. (9)

So we can see that industrial relations are not just about worker and employer. There are three parties - the union, the employer and the government. The government sets the laws to control the power of the unions. But it should also set the laws to control the responsibility and powers of the employers. In terms of art, the government should regulate the art market to help decide the value of an artist's work, how much galleries should pay artists (usually a % of sales) and also the price range the art should sell for. However, the government determining who is a good artist is problematic because of political agendas that they set. An Artists Union is better placed for this.

Groups, like the Royal Academy, or the Royal Association of British Sculptors function like a "closed shop" based on exclusivity and keep other artists out without explanation or feedback. The Royal Academy operates on an aristocratic exclusivity basis. In the words of Marx (Groucho) "I wouldn't want to belong to a club that would have me as a member." This is in contrast to the Artists Union of England's open membership. The Royal Academy has just 80 members, with new members elected following recommendation from other members. employers will only consider employing RA artists. This is problematic if the employers are the government commissions as it operates like a closed shop where the employer will only hire union members (or Royal Academicians) and those employees must remain members to remain employed. And according the Trade Union Labour Relations (Consolidation) Act 1992 a closed shop is not allowed. Galleries cannot be told to select artists from a list of union artists (closed shop). So why should it be different for the Royal Academy.

The Master & Servant Act of 1823 made it illegal (an imprison-able offence) for a worker to stop or change their job. The Employer was free to lay off workers and sue for damages if they went out on strike. (10) Now something similar can happen. For example, if an artist upsets a gallery then their reputation can be ruined without recourse. Artists can easily be replaced, there is a plentiful supply. Well paid engineers, with unique and sought after skills, formed the Amalgamated Society of Engineers and played a role in Trade Unions. But artists didn't have a similar union. Poor/Working Class "Artists" of the day, restricted from formal education had another unions such as the "Carpenters, Masons and Bricklayers." These unions included skilled workers, excluded from the status of being artists, but artists non-the-less. The artist's role was always too closely tied with the ruling Patrons and elites. This is why they formed the exclusive Royal Academy.

In the 1960s the Labour Party proposed that workers must take part in decision-making at all levels. And that employers must negotiate and agree with Trades Union representatives. But also that employees need control and self-management in industry. (11) Currently only industry and government insider artists take part in decision making. And the Government art administrators help to keep artists from having a fair status. This occurs even in the language that they use. They use the term "emerging artist". But this implies that the other artists are "submerged". Artist should not accept these put down terms. It should be replaced by "favoured" (to administrators), and "un-favoured". Artists should be able to determine themselves whether their work has emerged. Artists are given administrative levels. We need to self-determine how we are "recognised" and not use the term "emerging" or mid-level. It patronises other artists into being seen as "submerged". Perhaps based on length of time being an artist rather than how long galleries have been interested in the artist, or the degree of interest that galleries have. Artists should be allowed to define if they have emerged as artists in their own practice.

3. FINANCE

FINANCE AND VALUE

After years in the art industry I believe that the value of cultural capital, reward and valuing is often greater than financial remuneration / reward. Financial reward creates value in a small selection of work from artists that belong to a certain demographic (often selected from a gallerist or buyers pure subjectivity and without transparency and based in nepotism and cronyism). Proving this is difficult because there is no audit trail that can be easily accessed.

I hope to generate a union based appreciation of art that isn't linked to the corporate finance world whose bankers, property investors and lawyers appear to dominate the selection of artwork. This union based approach will fit in with union history and have its own history and counter narrative to the current monopoly (hegemony) of corporate art.

DEFINING THE CLASS SYSTEM

The identity of the traditional working class has been destroyed by the political and economic decisions professional elite with the removal of many key industries. And a significant portion of the former Middle Class around the UK is now educated but poor and non-working. Meanwhile, the London Upper and Middle, Rich and Comfortable Classes are out of touch with the rest of the country because they are the ones privileged to get the work.

The distinction of working class, middle class and ruling class no longer applies. Many people traditionally in the working class are now unemployed or an underclass. People in the ruling classes like to point to the fact that they work as hard as people in the working classes, to co-opt the title "working class". I propose these 3 new systems that interrelate. None of the class system makes anyone better than anyone else. It is about features of peoples' lives, not the people themselves. There is also no assumption that art by anyone's of a certain class is better than that of anyone else. The people are judged as equal as people and their art is judged on its own terms. For example, my father, Donald Padgett, whose became a ceramic artist in his retirement, was unqualified in art yet sold more work at the Cumbria Sculptors exhibitions than academically qualified members of the Cumbria Sculptors group. At the next committee meeting, for some reason, the group leaders decided to change policy and only allow membership renewal to those with an art qualification, thus preventing my father from further participation.

1)   Lower, Middle and Upper Class. This is a value based system. Based on culture and education levels. It is a generalisation and can apply to different cultural areas. For example someone might be upper class about social etiquettes or wines and yet be lower class about art or motor mechanics and vice-versa.

2)   Poor, Comfortable and Rich Class. This is an economic based system. Based on finances and assets level. Often a person's financial status gives them greater cultural status than they deserve. The phrase "Whoever pays the piper calls the tune" translates into the fallacy of "whoever pays for the art decides what is good art." Whilst this is true for what is good art in their subjective opinion it is not objectively true.

3)   Non-working and Working Class. This is an activity based system. Based on whether a person is in an employment (this can include volunteer and low level remuneration self-employed) or non-employment (can be unemployed or leisured or retired).

According to this system we can now have nuance to have an Upper Class, Poor, Working person, e.g. a PhD student or a person from an aristocratic family that went bankrupt, and their opposite a Lower Class, Rich, Non-Working Person, e.g. a person who won the pools. Most artists, I would suggest, are Middle Class, Poor and Working. However, there are a number of highly advantaged Upper Class, Rich and Working artists who make use of social and economic connections that the majority of artists do not have. Nepotism and cronyism can occur in the buying and selling of art and also in the selecting of artists by other artists for exhibitions and studio space. Without a clear critical framework these corruptions are a lazy fall-back position to take when making decisions.

It is also interesting that at a time when 94% of artists supported remaining in the European Union (12) that so few want to join an Artists' Union. Perhaps this being a London Centred and comfortable middle class response as opposed to a poor lower class response. But that said, union membership has declined and this is possibly in part due to the fact that many causes, such as a an 8 hour day, a 40 hour week etc have been won and are now taken for granted.

Artists are uniquely positioned between the rich and middle wage classes and also poor workers and the unemployed. Artists often have to take low-skilled work to survive or are from wealthy families. The benefit of this is that it gives an artist's union potential access to all classes of society.

An important note about these characterisations is that they appear to be split into thirds and the upper and rich appear to behave as if they are entitled to at least a third of representation and influence. Whereas the proportion of upper and rich class is significantly smaller than that of lower and poor.

MERITOCRACY – CLASS AND DISCRIMINATION

The Panic! Survey into Social Class, Taste and Inequalities was research by a team of academics from the Universities of Edinburgh and Sheffield, funded by the Arts and Humanities Research Council. P4 This research in the Creative Industries showed three areas of belief in how artists could progress in their careers; meritocracy (including talent, ambition and hard work), social networks (including who you know, family background, wealth, gender and ethnicity) and education (both people's own and their parents).

The Panic! Survey showed that upper middle class men were "overrepresented compared to the overall numbers of upper middle class origin and working class origin in the labour force as a whole." (13) that the most influential people in the creative industries who are in the best placed to effect change believe most strongly in meritocracy and are "also most sceptical of the impact of social factors, such as gender, class or ethnicity, on explanations for success in the sector." (14)

"34.8% of the creative workforce in London are from upper-middle class origins."(15)

"Currently, a key characteristic of the British cultural and creative workforce is the absence of those from working class social origins."(16)
And that this "intersects with other characteristics, primarily gender and ethnicity. Women, and those from Black and Minority Ethnic (BAME) communities face barriers in addition to those associated with social class origin."(17)

On social networks the report states "These explanations point to barriers in the cultural sector, so that no matter how talented or hard working someone is, they will still struggle if they aren't part of the same class, ethnicity, and/or gender as the people hiring and promoting them." (18)

And on education the report states "Research shows a strong relationship between someone's level of education and their abilities, but also finds that people from middle class homes have better access to elite educational institutions." (19) It later states that cultural tastes play an important role in getting into upper-middle class occupations. Hiring can be a form of 'cultural matching', excluding those who do not have the shared tastes of specific social groups. This is especially true in cultural and creative occupations and is

another important and subtle barrier for those seeking to work in the sector."
(20)

FINANCE DICTATING ART

Art has become a luxury activity. Like expensive cars and houses. Artists may be poor but feel rich because they engage in a luxury activity. Art that is not about money – but it is an activity of money and privilege. Alternative non-economic art activities have been created but they often have their own propaganda elements that limit their scope and do not get promoted in the moneyed system.

Most artists spend days and weeks on work that sells for a fraction of the cost in time that it takes to make. When I am asked how long did a painting take to paint. It may have taken 3 hours but it also took 51 years for me to be in the place to know what to do. Artists are self-employed workers who provide "goods" for sale. But legislation only covers performance and so goods should be considered in terms of the performance inherent within them. The life history of the artists that they put into the work. They do not produce widgets on the factory floor but physical pieces of meaning and value.

Art is not a job, it's a vocation and how much money you make is not the only thing. But when you tell people you are an artist they usually ask how much you make, do you make a living, do you sell much work or are you famous. Perhaps better questions are what kind of work do you make, what is your work about, or what inspires you.

DO YOU MAKE A LIVING FROM ART?

The question "do you make a living from doing art?" is often the first question that I am asked when I say that I am an artist. The question is inconsiderate. If the artist does make a living then the questioner will be impressed although largely un- interested. The artist will feel proud and justified. If they don't then the questioner is still largely uninterested. But they can then be internally dismissive. The artist then feels undermined and undervalued. If you say that you don't make a living then they think your work isn't good enough and also if you are still an artist then you are wasting your time or sponging off the state.

I would suggest that around 99% of artists don't make a living so 99% of the times this is asked it will leave the artist feeling undermined and undervalued. It is also a power question, allowing the asker to put the artist into a position of being controlled economically. The questioner feels economically superior because they are allowing their value system to be asserted over the artist. It is a way to see what your status in art is and also to locate you into the economic based class system. It is also if they feel outside of the cultural class system then they are able to relocate you into an economic based system and assert their superiority over you.

For me art is not a job, it's a vocation and how much money you make is not the only thing. But when you tell people you are an artist they usually ask how much you make, do you make a living, do you sell much work or are you famous. Perhaps better questions are what kind of work do you make, what is your work about, or what inspires you.

A small number of artists make a living from art, yet without all the other competing artists the small number wouldn't exist and there would be no artistic development. For the majority of artists, it costs more to make artwork than it sells for. In the current gallery system artists do not get the true value of their work. And it is not just the time that it takes to make each individual work but also that the style and ideas going into the work are developed over the life of the artist.

The gallerist selling the artist's work, often correctly, believe that they have created the value of the art and that artist. They know that they could have chosen almost anyone to promote. And artists who do make a living from art are then able to assert their superiority in the artistic system by failing to recognise this superiority is economic and not necessarily artistic.

Funding, grants and commissions received by artists are often for small amounts (the largest portions of the funds to individuals going to wages for the administrators who distribute the money). These small amounts often go to artists who are middle class and can afford to survive without the funds. Their main benefit is to be able to promote the fact that they have funding from an approved body (such as the Arts Council England).

Art has never been about money for me. Although I am constantly told it should be by non-artists or artists who go along with the system. I fund myself through teaching and create the work that I believe in. Like myself, many artists have a different system of capital. It is not just about money. It is more like old craftsmanship which gave a sense of satisfaction and contribution to a wider society and wider causes (whether religious, political or social), whilst also allowing the craftsperson to be respected and comfortable in society. This was before the alienation of the craftsperson from the production of their craft items by putting these craftspeople into factories.

Whilst art can be for consumption by consumers this is not its only role. Art can also be not for consumption, is designed not to be palatable, not to reinforce standard viewpoints. This is what makes it Avant Garde. It is designed to challenge. When challenge is a pretence then it is Trans-Avant-Garde. When it is accepted by the established commercial order it is Trans-Avant-Garde. Using this notion is the way that curators in the artworld have created a theoretical model that allows them to take no notice of dissent outside the Trans-Avant-Garde. When they only see "real" artists as ironic in their protests and just self-interested or based in commerciality it means they can choose to address only the issues they want to address. It reflects their own interests and the cynicism towards those with other perspectives.

The "Me Too" movement against sexual harassment and the "Extinction Rebellion" movement against Climate Change are both movements embraced in artistic circles – and only become problematic for curators when they protest against the gallery corporate funders). But protests that do not fit the curators' moralities or which challenge the art establishment (such as my Religious Discrimination Employment Tribunal Case against the Tate Galleries in 2005) are largely ignored. And when issues are addressed it is by looking at symptoms, e.g. sex or race discrimination incidents, rather than the systemic cause i.e. non-accountable selection systems. They are stuck within this art system and can't see outside it.

Art was outside of the rules but now the rules are broken and we are all just footnotes in the history of art. Artists like Banksy are political about issues and themes many in the artworld agree with but not about the real structures of art. They don't challenge these. For instance Banksy's stencil art has extreme similarities to the French graffiti artist Blek le Rat. whilst Blek le Rat is a respected figure the two artists who are not promoted to the same level. Banksy admits an influence but does not appear to call for change of status for artists to be appropriately respected for their influence and originality.

There is a difference between academic, union, popular and commercial art. You cannot dictate what people want to buy, but just because people want to buy it doesn't make it art. You also cannot dictate what academics want to write about, but just because academics write about something, that writing doesn't make it art. Union Art should be what has been systematically established as art. And because people with a strong focus on narrative systems of value don't always see the importance of purely formal qualities of art, a union needs to consciously put aside its moral and political purposes for art so that it can clearly see the purely formal qualities of art. When it knows what good art is then it can harness those qualities in creating works that also have a message.

DEMOCRACY

Art is currently like a dictatorship. Art is Elitist and exclusive, it is about how many you can keep out of the "club" rather than about how many you can get into the "club". But there is a false dichotomy between art exclusivity and democracy. The problem isn't that Art is upper class, or Elitist (in the sense of being educated, informed, rational and sensitive) but that it is "Elitist" in a biased and unaccountable way. It is run by incompetent people who are snobbish and abuse their power. In contrast the Union should not be mob rule with group selection by mass consent. Selection needs to be by use of educated standards and criteria to select with clarity. It needs stating if artwork is issue based.

The lower/poorer classes are still producing artworks, just aren't being recognised for them. The recognition is being given to the Elite. Many artistic geniuses are not recognised because they are one of the many artists who lay the ground work for the promoted/recognised/key artists.

An Economics Class Consciousness of Art sees that there is a moral issue to the importance of art. Is it so important or just a formal and almost academic activity that has been hijacked to promote particular propaganda values? We are told that it is a high aspiration. This is part of an economic control, and the majority of people will never be let into the system anyway. It keeps people aiming at something that they can never achieve. It is important, but not so important to make heroes out of artists in order to keep artisans and crafts people from having any status.

POPULISM

This is not Art for All – as what kind of art do "All" want. Is art to be tailored to the market but what is art still needs qualifying within mass appeal. Low quality art is like a diet of fish and chips. You can't stop people buying fish and chips (art) but as chefs / artists you can let people know that what they are buying is low quality food / low quality art. Populism and democracy in art can also become the way to decide what is good art. Art is by nature elitist but should be fair and meritocratic. "Fish and chip" representational art is a game of spot the difference (between reality and the image created). Abstract art is still a game of understand the difference. But using a different language. Fascist art and communist state narrative art were representation. Revolutionary art was opposed to this. Artists avoid being defined by the ordinary public who do not understand and who cannot afford to buy art-works.

SUBJECTIVE BIAS

The problem simply stated; if art is allowed to be just subjective then the wealthy people will buy art that reflects their values rather than the intrinsic values of an artwork or the values of arts. And the values of people with money often is money – and not art or some other cause that art might be appropriated to.

With a disproportionate (compared to the rest of society) number of wealthy people and leaders in business are psychopaths (as accords the psychological definition) and if art is selected, bought and promoted by these people then it is clear that their mental health is distorting what is judged to be art. The artists should be allowed to determine what they think is art. However, if the majority of artists are also psychopaths then the difference might be negligible.

And "Fake Art" is hard to spot as art is directed by sales mixed with some critique. The critique can be made by those in favour of traditional art or in favour of contemporary art. Whatever the dealer's own subjective taste coupled with what approach they think will sell the work.

ECONOMIC SYSTEMS

The above is not to categorise the artist as a kind of moral or religious figure. Artists are traders as well as cultural/meaning generators. Both have a place. Cultural value is enhanced by the sales and promotion and the sales having significance through the cultural value. The danger is who determines what value that should be promoted – the sales person or the artist.

In "The Wealth of Nations" (1776) Adam Smith set a philosophical and economic model of market forces. Yet what were the market rewards for his mother who brought him up and the family unit outside the state system. Benefits are used to pay families. Families buy products and services through taxes. Taxes pay for infrastructure and for the development of customers. The end users of art could pay a tax that is then paid to artists – e.g. Galleries could pay a tax and not just allow artists reduced entry as the latter only benefit the artist living in the cities. Artist can then be paid a special benefit of some kind. There are other forms of economic reward. And although they might not be not financial care must still be taken that there isn't corruption.

Art is a currency but its true value should be determined by artists and not by financiers. Art has value to artists and has value (a price) to investors. The two are not the same. If money is seen as most important then the investors give the true value. If the artist's value is most important then the money value is part of a secondary system. Just because people with money buy an artwork it doesn't make it good art. Unless their choices are informed as it is just what the people with money want to buy.

And who are the art employers? As well as individual patrons there are state supporters and patrons. The art market economy is not laissez-faire as there is state intervention with funders like the Arts Council England. However, rather than having members of the general public, or general artists the people selected for being on public art finance committees belong to the small portion of art buying public and this reinforces the distortion of art.

The collection and validation processes is often based on prejudice and whim, with selectors have no or limited training, understanding and experience in art and how artists live. Human error is endemic.

PAYMENT

The AUE and Unions in general have a focus on payment. However, focus on payment, in art, continues the oppression. It allows the level and status of art to be dictated by how much is paid for the art and artists. Pay is a method of controlling artists. Only those who are paid can make artwork. Artist should still make work to prevent themselves from being ignored. For example, if the wealthy in society are racist against a racial minority then they would not pay for art from that minority. However, that non-payment would not diminish the work of those artists.

AUE require fair wages yet ask their artists to work as volunteers. This is an apparent contradiction. It requires that the union value volunteer work. Therefore they must have a policy on when and where it is acceptable. Which has been the case for unions since their creation, that they require workers to work for no remuneration to help the Union cause. Members of the Artists Union leadership asked me to be a representative and asked if I would do this on a voluntary (i.e. unpaid) capacity. This shows that the issue of pay is not crucial for a union. In fact I believe it keeps the artist focussed on being in low pay jobs rather than getting the higher status commissions. According to my 3 factor class system I would be a middle class, comfortable, worker. This means that I am able to do the voluntary work.

The Panic! Survey showed "For those from working class backgrounds who were interviewed, unpaid work was seen as inescapable and a form of exploitation. Those from upper-middle class origins expressed the same weight of expectation to work for free but were more likely to describe the potential career benefits of unpaid work."(21) The Survey also found that the working class origin people (compared to the other classes) "do not seem to be benefitting from working for free as a way of accessing their desired occupation." (22)

As many artists no longer need to be paid (due to many being already rich or having alternative incomes) the way to progress in art has ceased to be through a fair remuneration system. Unions should host or fund art and exhibitions as an act of cultural liberty and defiance. Making art and its fair valuation is a political act that unions should support. If there is the capability (and Artificial Intelligence in computers now allows for the capability – see chapter 5) everyone should be entitled to have their art viewed and assessed as a matter of a human right of freedom of expression and right of reply. And with fair assessment fair remuneration should follow.

THE CRITICS AND GALLERIES

And what about objectivity from critics, galleries, academics and teachers. They all exploit artists and students to some degree by making a living out of them. And this is done despite many of the exploiters being artists themselves. Genuine art criticism doesn't exist. What we have is art rhetoric. It is more like poetry but even poetry has criticism and so should art and writing about art.

At Schools, Art Colleges and Universities students are told to keep the work that shows the development of their ideas. It is implied that this is to show how you have come to your work. And there is the assumption that sometime, someone will be interested in this. And that you might be able to use this information to show how your work came before another artist's work if that artists becomes famous for that style. But there is nowhere to go if someone else does your style of work. The gallery promoting the artist probably won't want to take notice, or will find an excuse as to why their artist is subtly different. Either way, it is unlikely that you would get a reply from them. Copyright Law won't apply unless your work is an exact copy. And at present there is no other regulatory body to help.

Pulitzer Prize award winning New York Art Critic Jerry Saltz says that the appreciation of art is from a basic reaction like the basic reaction people have towards music. That it can't be analysed, just like music can't be analysed. However, we do analyse music. (23)

Key critics and curators such as Tim Marlow state that originality should not be a primary concern for artists – showing that there is a culture of disregard for complaints of theft of artistic intellectual property. He states that artists should make work they believe in rather than work to sell, and that galleries will then sell that work. However, he doesn't suggest ways for critics and curators to select this kind of work in a fair process. (24)

Artists and dealers think it is acceptable to "steal" other artists work and not make attribution. It is part of the ethos of rich and commercially successful and socially connected artists and galleries to steal off poorer artists. Whilst I cannot provide a quote for this I have heard artists say it many times. It was Steve Jobs who said, in 1996, that Picasso had a saying ""good artists copy; great artists steal" -- and we (Apple) have always been shameless about stealing great ideas." (25) Picasso never said that and his name was stolen by Jobs to make a point, although it is true that his work was influence by other artists like George Braque. Similarly Vincent Van Gogh's style was heavily influenced by other artists work, e.g. the cloisonnism of Emile Bernard. Yet even though these sources might be acknowledged they are ignored by dealers, buyers, artists and the public.

Critics and artists perpetuate that selling work is the aim. It is hard to separate critical and artistic acclaim. Magnus Resch, Ph.D., is an art market economist who in 2016 started the Magnus App (http://www.magnus.net) which works like Shazam for Art. If you photograph artworks on your mobile phone it is able to identify themand provide you with information about the works. He also created Larry's list (https://www.larryslist.com) as an internet based rich list in art. For a fee you are able to discover the contact details of art buyers and dealers. The site reinforces all the prejudices in art being a financial activity. And because so much money is involved in art that is why there should be regulation. And whilst Magnus Resch states that there needs to be transparency in art, for him transparency doesn't mean public accountability in decision making, it meant putting price levels on artworks so that people could see the prices easily and decide whether to buy the work or not. (26)

Academics were the gatekeepers for the art system. Now respected academics write about what the rich pay for as art, whether it is artistically significant or not. Those selling art often compromise their values to sell what pays. The people in this close relationship between the rich and the artworld can be called the "artistocracy". However, there is a danger of developing a constant focus on the narratives of Transactional Analysis. In this the Victim has low wages. The Rescuer calls for wage standards. And the Persecutor is the person insisting that artists and galleries need to follow the standards. We need a way forward that is Win-Win for artists, gallery, buyer and government.

My proposals are all product led. If they were market led I would ask: what do the artists and galleries want in terms of regulation. This would give a more inconsistent perspective based out of differences of opinion that might not address the broader issues in the essay.

SELF-PUNISHMENT

Because art is pretended to be a meritocracy it also means that artists, wrongly, blame themselves, their art or their networking skills, if they do not become an artistic success (which has been conflated with being a financial success). This is the final cruel twist. It is hard for artists to face up to this and so they suppress or reject thoughts and the feelings of inadequacy. And so the inequality remains unexpressed consciously and consequently remains unchallenged externally.

4. REGULATION

Regulation of Art is not to be confused with the regulation of business. Art is not business. The two are connected but also distinct. And there should also be a regulation of the Art Business (as well as a regulation of Art). Regulation comes out of selection criteria for art and unfortunately it is fashionable for the majority of artists, curators and critics to deny that criteria are possible to apply in art. They seem to claim that art is subjective. And hide behind this claim when making selection of artwork. Often selecting unoriginal and derivative art mistaking it for the opposite. Part of the reason why people believe art is purely subjective may be that they feel overwhelmed by the task of seeking objectivity. Yet I believe that the development of artificial intelligence and algorithms will change this. And my system also allows for subjectivity by giving each entry a quality rating and allowing that people can still have personal preference for one work over another) but puts subjectivity within objective parameters. The system allows good and bad art to be determined more easily and original art to be identified.

SYSTEMS TO ENSURE ART SELECTION IS FAIR

As well as subjective impulses (often built over a life-time of building prejudices) art selection and promotion is often based on academic, commercial (gallery) and institutional (museum and gallery) connections. There is no unified art discourse. Without this there is no systematic selection. Selection should be systematised for fairness so that feedback for improvement can be given. Systems allow feedback. With fair selection comes fair remuneration.

People commissioning and selecting art are often not qualified to do so and need to be qualified. Selection should also be by qualified selectors, and often it can be by people with little or no experience of qualification. The commercial world affects decisions by institutions and institutions affect the academic reputations world.

Why select one artist's work over another's. To prevent corrupt / biased selection clear criteria are required. Criteria for selecting work needs to be transparent.

The people who are best able to select work are the artists, not the financiers. The artists wouldn't tell the financiers how to run their businesses. So why would financiers think that they could tell artists what was good art. A focus on money as a source of value feeds into the capitalist system and mentality.

REGULATION

Regulation comes out of systems. You can't have regulation without a system to be the standard to work towards. Regulation is an antithesis of artistic freedom. But it is needed for the promotion and understanding of art. Artists don't want their freedom restricting and fail to realise that regulation will increase their freedom. Artists need to justify their work or have a curator or gallerist justify it. There is a conflation between artistic freedom and curatorial/dealer freedom as whilst artists should have freedom to create, the curators should be regulated and controlled in what they promote as being art. The artist is responsible for individual expression whereas the curator is responsible for the positioning of the individual expressions within a system of value judgment. Regulation and grading of what is and is not art give consumer protection. As well as protecting other artists from having their work (original ideas and styles) stolen or overlooked.

Whatever regulation is created artists will want to break the regulation and create work outside of it. Art is party about breaking boundaries. When there are no boundaries (as is supposedly the case in current art) how can new art be created. A critical system allows boundaries to be put back in place. And after they are put in place then they can be broken.

After studying an MA in Theory of Contemporary Art and Performance Practice I was surprised that there is no unified body of art theory. There are disjointed assertions from a number of artists and critics but no objective criteria. What is supposed to be art theory is really just a history of art, describing what happened, rather than analysing what makes something an artwork. Analysis often is based on an agenda such as socialism or feminism. These gain credence in academic circles but the art market continues on the basis of the views, tastes and whims of a few influential buyers.

The buyer or artist is very prone to buying or producing non-art in the mistaken belief that it is art. And to hide behind the lack of standards and critical analysis in art contemporary art dealers have defined that it is impossible to define art. In doing this they have failed to realize their own self-contradiction. In my book "ART: How To View Understand And Criticise Modern, Contemporary And Traditional Art Works" I created a system to help people pick through what is actually original in art. It is the beginnings of categories for an algorithm and perhaps we will eventually have artificial intelligence helping show us what is original art. (27)

As an art historian and theoretician I investigated how artwork is listed in electronic museum management systems and how art gallery collections. I found the taxonomy (terms used) involved thousands of terms that are so specific that they are completely unwieldy. These taxonomies are useful for cataloguing what is already accepted as art. But not for analysing and challenging whether those works are actually art. Simpler dictionary definitions present art terms, art movements and techniques that are too specific. Their terms e.g. Cubism and Bricolage, are composed of a number of different features. This makes it hard to analyse and cross reference works because their features are not broken down into constituent parts. The advantage of having a list of the constituent parts of a style of art then you can describe an art movement, such as Cubism and Futurism and clearly see what they have in common.

So I hung 500 copies of artworks from the history of art in my studio space and systematically categorised them. Not according to art movements, but according to what I saw, phenomenologically, i.e. how things appear. To be of value this system needed to be turned into a usable project. So I created a table of categories and values. The resulting system of categorisation is a work of art in itself but the next step was to apply the system in analysing museum and gallery collections for the better understanding of art in museums. The system looks at stylistic form only. Any thematic content, e.g. love, war, flowers, castles, can be analysed separately.

My system accounts for how a work can be not formally originally yet can be of a high quality and that people might see it as art. And the same analysis can be applied to contemporary pieces. They may look original, but very similar works have been done before – e.g. Hirst's "The Physical Impossibility of Death in the Mind of Someone Living" 1991 having similarities to Jeff Koon's earlier "One Ball Total Equilibrium Tank" 1985. Or Tracey Emin's "My Bed" 1998 having similarities to Louise Bourgoise's earlier "Red Room Parents" 1994. Another e.g. Claus Oldenburgh large sculptures of household objects e.g. "Lipstick (Ascending) on Caterpillar Tracks" 1969. These are like renaissance still life paintings or sculptures. The only difference is that they are larger and of modern items and of modern materials. But in essence they are representational artworks.

ARTWORK SYSTEM TO PROPERLY DETERMINED WORK AS ART

Some formal styles of work are more appropriate to some semantic contents, e.g. sensual bodies and curves, machines and angles. These styles and contents can be mixed to artistic effect, e.g. sensual bodies shown with angles or machines with curves. Thus artistic form mixing with content can provide new combinations but the system allows for this, just prevents very detailed content being seen as artistically innovative, rather than as Propaganda (not innovative art with an added message). This is important as it is easier to have an innovative message than an innovative artistic style.

Art that is promoted as greater art than it is can be called "Fake Art" as it is like "Fake News". Fake Art is not just art that's a copy of another work but arts that pretends to have a higher artists status than it deserves. If something is stated to be derived from, or a copy of, other work then we know what it is.

Systems/regulations are also required to ensure an artwork system is followed. Then the properly determined art can chosen for exhibition or promotion. Using methodologies for art selection allows the artists union to give its seal of approval and authenticity, rather than this come from just commerce or the academy or state galleries. This is not to propose the union as the only voice but a significant one that affects the value (not necessarily the price) of works. If a selection is justified to a union then that transparency would give the union more credibility than the corporate art world. There is also a difference between quality of what artists create using techniques other artists have discovered and the innovation artists make. Someone can invent a style that is new but their works don't have aesthetic appeal. And others can create great quality aesthetic works using those techniques.

REGULATING ARTISTS

In order to gain support for a regulatory system the first people that need regulating are the artists themselves in relation to their behaviour towards each other. Examples like artists cliques and their bullying of other artists occurs. And stealing ideas of other artists. And artists bragging about their exhibitions and levels of funding. This all contributes to a civil service like structure for artists careers that is unsurprisingly perpetuated by the government's arts civil service, the Arts Council England . Giving exhibition opportunities to friends. This is why the critic and the gallerist should be seen as regulatory of artists. But with that comes a responsibility that the critic and the gallerist have failed to fulfil this. So now is the time for artists need to get their relations in order before determining how to relate to galleries and institutions.

Often morals will be part of the content of art but can also be part of the materials and form of art. These morals of art also need regulating to ensure that there isn't encouragement for something to be created as art just because it hasn't been done before due to its being morally questionable e.g. using dead bodies or body parts - like the 2002 blockbuster Body Worlds anatomy exhibition in London where corpses (who had been dissected or whose skin had been peeled off) had been impregnated with plastic (using Professor Gunther von Hagens technique) and were then exhibited in lifelike poses.

For change to occur, artists first will need to recognise the need for systems to fairly assess their work and the work of other artists. Artists can get ratings according to the quality of their work. And whilst everyone has a right to call themselves an artist not everyone has the right to call themselves a good artist. And whilst there is difference between curating community art and high gallery art this should not lead to prejudice about the quality in one rather than the other. Art is about equality and not just how many shows you've been accepted for. It is about the quality of the shows and your work within those shows.

5. ARTIFICIAL INTELLIGENCE

When Helen Legg, Director of Tate Liverpool gave a talk at the Birley Studios in Preston in August 2019 about the open call for applications for "Art North West " for a Northern artist to put on a solo show at Tate Liverpool, she said that a tick box exercise is too time consuming for each application. However, it is an unconsidered excuse to suggest that you would tick boxes for each person. The boxes are a framework and when familiar with the framework they can be mentally ticked almost instantaneously. Many of these factors are already in operation but in a hidden and unjustified way. Artists could also tick the boxes for their own applications. Whilst this Director dismissed the idea with incredulity (and it was demonstrated in the Panic Report that people in positions of power and authority in the arts disproportionately feel that they, and those around them, achieve their positions through a meritocracy) it is the future. But not human curators, rather Artificial Intelligence can tick many of the boxes. A framework rounds decisions and justifies choices. They give transparency.

It is intellectually lazy not to create the categories. Curators are often given the task of analysing an artist's work because some artists can't or don't want to do it. Therefore curators should be able to do this. Their job is to articulate what artists can't articulate. For an artist (or their curator) to say that they don't need to do this is to not fulfil their duty and responsibility. Artists or curators should point out why an artist's work is original or of quality in a given format (whether figurative, abstract or conceptual etc). Artists, curators and people in general seem very convinced that an art system cannot happen, without entertaining the possibility that it can. They are prejudicial against a system and they show a lack of open-mindedness. Other myths that are current are that nothing new can be created in art, and that it is alright to steal another artists' work.

Database of artists and justification of why there work is or is not art.

Database of curators and galleries who show good practice and bad practice.

DATABASES, COMPUTER ARTIFICIAL INTELLIGENCE AND COMPUTER LEARNING.

It doesn't matter if the majority of artists or curators are led by finance as the change will come through Artificial Intelligence programs. Computers are going to decide what is quality, innovative and original art. Already programmers have designed Artificial Intelligence to sort images of paintings into historical order based on formal qualities and without any pre-knowledge of that historical order.

"Several studies have shown the ability of the machine to learn and predict style categories, such as Renaissance, Baroque, Impressionism, etc., from images of paintings. This implies that the machine can learn an internal representation encoding discriminative features through its visual analysis. However, such a representation is not necessarily interpretable. We conducted a comprehensive study of several of the state-of-the-art convolutional neural networks applied to the task of style classification on 77K images of paintings, and analyzed the learned representation through correlation analysis with concepts derived from art history. Surprisingly, the networks could place the works of art in a smooth temporal arrangement mainly based on learning style labels, without any a priori knowledge of time of creation, the historical time and context of styles, or relations between styles. The learned representations showed that there are few underlying factors that explain the visual variations of style in art." (28).

And already there has been an algorithm to determine whose work, of 6 composers, was the most original.

"Scientists in South Korea have built an algorithm which they claim is capable of judging objectively the extent to which 19 of the best known composers brought the art form forward. They developed a computer model which divided each of the musicians' compositions into "codewords", which were then used to compare hundreds of pieces of music both against the composers' previous works and the wider cannon. It found Sergei Rachmaninoff, a giant of the late Romantic period, scored the highest, followed by J.S. Bach, Brahms and Mendelssohn." (29)

An art union needs to be engaged and spearheading in the computer revolution so that it can protect artists' reputations and work. A.I. is being used to determine if artworks are fakes based on brushwork.

"In a new paper, researchers from Rutgers University and the Atelier for Restoration & Research of Paintings in the Netherlands document how their system broke down almost 300 line drawings by Picasso, Matisse, Modigliani, and other famous artists into 80,000 individual strokes. Then a deep recurrent neural network (RNN) learned what features in the strokes were important to identify the artist."..."The most significant use of AI in art may be the much less sensational role of sorting out controversies over who painted what in situations where forgery is not in question. Art history is more complex than we think. As Subramanian notes, great artists might paint the same theme several times, students or other artists might fill in paintings, and lesser artists might copy the work, maybe changing it. Machine learning systems, trained on hundreds of images, can spot tiny similarities that identify a style and thus tell a story of composition:" (30)

This detection of fakes is being harnessed to protect investments by Dr. Carina Popovici and Christiane Hoppe-Oehl at https://art-recognition.com/ however it also needs harnessing to promote artists rewards. It is similar to the regulation of the use of personal data in with artists' artworks as their personal data. They are their copyright, intellectual property and personal data. As significant to their being used without permission is their being excluded from being used. Any use of AI to determine validity should require the statement of what selection of work has been used. So that exclusions can be seen and justified.

ARTIFICIAL INTELLIGENCE AS ART

A.I. can include a science of subjectivity. The psychology of vision, statistics of what people like in an artwork. And eventually machines will also make sophisticated artworks, e.g. already a number of paintings done by computer have been found indistinguishable from the work of professional artists

"We proposed a system for generating art with creative characteristics. We demonstrated a realization of this system based on a novel creative adversarial network. The system is trained using a large collection of art images from the 15th century to 21st century with their style labels. The system is able to generate art by optimizing a criterion that maximizes stylistic ambiguity while staying within the art distribution. The system was evaluated by human subject experiments which showed that human subjects regularly confused the generated art with the human art, and sometimes rated the generated art higher on various high-level scales." (31)

This is a beginning as the programs are still unable to provide complex representational images.

"One of the main characteristics of the proposed system is that it learns about the history of art in its process to create art. However it does not have any semantic understanding of art behind the concept of styles. It does not know anything about subject matter, or explicit models of elements or principle of art. The learning here is based only on exposure to art and concepts of styles. In that sense the system has the ability to continuously learn from new art and would then be able to adapt its generation based on what it learns." (32)

However the development of facial recognition software shows that recognition and generation software for various human and animal forms are very possible. And systems of categorisation can also be used as a system of creation by computer. Future art can be made by a personal computer and be based on mood and scientific/psychological colour reactions. Would that be art if not by a human, or would the real artist be the programmers or the programmers over the years who laid the groundwork that led to the final program.

SYNDICALISM

I am not proposing "syndicalism" where the whole of an industry (art) is controlled by the workers (artists). Rather, I believe that computers will control art. And if artists don't control the computers then the customers (galleries and governments) will. This latter would probably mean that art would be made about what non-artists want it to be about. Rather than what artists want it to be about and rather than it just be about art itself. It would most likely mean that artworks were not fairly evaluated, just judged on what the public liked or on what sold to art buyers.

Art's propaganda (social and political) use is another aspect that needs to be seen separately. A system to determine originality and innovation in new cultural and thematic issues can be added to the purely formal system. Any system needs to first determine the formal qualities of a work of art and then its narrative, political and social meanings. An analysis of form and content can occur simultaneously by A.I. but unless formal qualities are separated at the outset and assigned greater value within a system (compared to any propaganda narratives) we will find dominant narratives will persist and minority artists (from other race, gender, sexuality, disability and religious values) will be ignored or have their work stolen by majority "Elite" artists.

For artists the issue of fair valuing of work needs to come first. And remuneration needs to come second. Without fair valuing a correct price for work can't be set.

Other computer systems for valuing work are possible. A regulation system on computer can have fluctuating "variables" like quality and originality that depend on what emphasis the person using the system would like to put on those variables. This would in part factor in subjectivity. With computing different variables can be programmed so that you can make multiple systems for what is original, what sells, what the public, like etc. There is no reason why the Union concerns can't develop alongside corporate and governmental concerns, all using the same A.I. systems.

RESISTANCE TO CHANGE

There is an inevitable resistance to regulations and an art register because it would remove the power bases of collectors, dealers and artists. It would destroy reputations, deflate over inflated prices and enable social mobility. We are told that there is a meritocracy in art but it doesn't exist, and there is no place to go when artists' work is appropriated by those in power.

Knowledge is the new economy. Automation has replaced blue collar manual labour – but is also replacing white collar mental labour. Products can be cheaply and endlessly reproduced and are readily available. Open source Wiki's (independent websites) should allow artists to upload works and create an alternative knowledge economy. The danger of this new economy is that it may remove the need or art dealers and curators and possibly even of the artists themselves.

ETHICAL ISSUES

Marnie Benney is the Head Curator at AIArtists.org in New York City and Pete Kistler is the Chief Technology Officer at www.AIArtists.org. They describe themselves as "a global clearinghouse of resources on AI's impact on art and culture, and the largest community of AI artists in the world." As well as the technical developments thy are interested in the ethical issues. Amongst some of their unanswered questions are issues of key concern to Artists' unions, particularly their "Dataset Challenges".

> "How can we prevent certain populations from being discriminated or marginalized by AI? Can we avoid providing unfair opportunity to certain groups based on training data? For example, hiring algorithms are often imbued with unknown biases that cause diversity and equal opportunity issues" (being explored by Joy Buolamwini) … "How can we ensure that the datasets used to train AI are fair and balanced? How can we prevent, understand, document and monitor bias built into our AI systems?" (being explored by Stephanie Dinkins)…"What missing datasets are holding back our human potential? ... For example, we lack a universal data source for civilian deaths from police, LGBTQ housing applicants who are denied (being explored by Mimi Onuoha)… "What are the consequences of unequal access to data? What does it mean that access trillions of data points about our every move are tracked and used by three main sources: governments, tech giants, and advertisers? " (33)

These issues all show how problems are passed on from real life to virtual life. There is an imminent danger of discrimination against minorities becoming systematised in the selection of artists and art professionals. And the problem will become deeper if A.I. systems become programmed by privileged minorities who use datasets (including art datasets) where minorities (and their art) are excluded. And this problem may become intractable if curators and programmers do not allow open access to art data due to issues of commercial sensitivity, intellectual property and copyright.

6. WAYS FORWARD

REVOLUTION

Will an Art revolution be like the Communist Revolution in Russia in 1917. There will be a regime change of the "Artistocracy" and many forces will seek to prevent the change. Corrupt forces within the change may also try to hijack the change for their own despotic ends. Alternative art histories will be possible at the touch of a button to select a variable (e.g. originality, women artists, black artist, etc.) And this concrete recognition of the subjectivity of history will engender tolerance and understanding. For it to work it may need heroic leaders, but ones who seek equality and egalitarianism.

Art People who posture and pretend to be "right on" but are self-righteous and self-serving present the greatest block to change as they don't see the problem and consequently don't believe it exists.
Nonetheless, the Art-world faced with artists armed with the internet is like the Catholic Church faced with seventeenth century Protestant Christians armed with their own printed bibles. A Protestant Reformation was the result for Christianity. Leaving two churches and centuries of development. And an artists' revolution based on artificial intelligence and databases is likely to cause an equivalent upheaval for the artworld.

METHODOLOGY FOR CREATING CHANGE

Theoretical frame gives an ideal that can then be used to approach a gallery for practical compromise and if compromise is acceptable. A practical measure to begin implementing good practice to transition into A.I. is that artists should begin to get feedback from galleries when submissions are rejected. And galleries shouldn't put open submissions if they can't give feedback. Detailed, workable, phased in implementation proposals will come from galleries making use of Artificial Intelligence systems. How these are controlled is an ethical issued that needs addressing, but the current system is unethical and it is no excuse to reject change by saying that it will be difficult to manage the ethics of a changed system.

Artist Union members should also seek to get into decision making roles with representatives in political arts committees in local and national government. On Government Committees and Government funded Galleries. On National Economic Development groups. Union members can be placed on committee boards if committees are union sympathetic or if unions can exert power. Art unions can also provide collective bargaining power and can then force committees to include their members on the board.

PAYMENT SYSTEMS

Instead of just one artist getting a wage we can have all artists paid a wage and people can select work after paying into a union art patron subscription system. This would remove "star" artists. This is unfair if there is a clear difference in the quality between 2 artists. Therefore after levels of art creation are created there also needs to be quality grading levels. These payment levels can be negotiated between employers, artists and the government. A database system can determine fair remuneration for use of images and works in exhibition, publication, etc.

It is important not to get trapped in a new Transactional Analysis model of Victim (Artist unfairly valued), Rescuer (Regulation of Art) and Persecutor (Union telling artists and galleries need to follow the regulations). In reality a Win-Win situation is needed, where artists, galleries, governments and consumers all work together for the mutual benefit and advancement of art.

HERE ARE SOME POSSIBLE FUTURE ACTIONS TO TAKE

IN RELATION TO ARTISTS

This is required before you make change in galleries. How artists act towards each other will give an example of how you would like galleries to behave towards other artists. This might require a Code of Conduct, or a Workers Charter of how to behave towards each other.

IN RELATION TO UNIONS

Upload artists work to wiki arts so they can be used in AI databases

Union Art Competition for exhibition at buildings like the TUC HQ London

Union Art Scheme – loan of artworks for union buildings.

Include "Artwork of the month" in Trade Union magazines

Encourage Union members to buy and collect art by members of the Artists Union.

ACTIONS TO TAKE IN RELATION TO ACADEMIC BODIES

Contact course tutors to give talks at Art Schools / Universities

Contact Students Unions to give talks.

ACTIONS TO TAKE IN RELATION TO EMPLOYERS

e.g. Commissioners, Galleries, Publishers, workshop programmers, media, curators .

Inform galleries that they have a rep for the artists Union – working for win-win in trade disputes.

Establish Artist Union accredited galleries.

Regulating curators with rating systems – to say how good the curators are and what kind of works they curate.

Require galleries to provide reasons for selecting and rejecting artworks.

Pro-forma letter of complaint and advice to send to organisations if you don't get a reply to an application.

Ask galleries for a policy statement on why struggling artist should pay submissions fees for exhibitions.

Union list for gallery grievances (Me Too for Art)

We can boycott exhibitions in public galleries. Don't pay to go to their exhibitions until they give artists discounts or select artist fairly. Historian Howard Zinn "Consumers have the power of the boycott, which is tantamount to the power of the strike in that they can bring a large corporation to its knees," We are in a "Corporatocracy" led by billionaires. (34)
We can boycott exhibitions in public galleries. Don't pay to go to them.

Picket galleries who are not looking after artists.

REFERENCES

1 Cogswell, David and Butzer, C.M. "Unions For Beginners", For Beginners LLC, 2012- p141
2 Cogswell, David and Butzer, C.M. Op. Cit. – p151
3 Cogswell, David and Butzer, C.M. Op. Cit. - p140
4 irch, Lionel "The History of the T.U.C. 1868 – 1968" The General Council of the Trades Union Congress, 1968 – p57
5 https://www.royalacademy.org.uk/page/a-brief-history-of-the-ra?gclid=EAIaIQobChMIxaeunr_q5wIVCLDtCh1KUQDYEAAYASAAEgIdj_D_BwE
6 Savage, Katharine "The Story of British Trade Unions", Kestrel Books 1977 - p14
7 Savage, Katharine. Op. Cit. – p45
8 Savage, Katharine. Op. Cit. – p64
9 Savage, Katharine. Op. Cit. – p137
10 Savage, Katharine. Op. Cit. - p70
11 Savage, Katharine. Op. Cit. – p126
12 Luke, Ben. Art Newspaper January 31st 2020 https://www.theartnewspaper.com/news/comment-or-crying-over-eu?utm_source=The+Art+Newspaper+Newsletters&utm_campaign=134ccc685e-EMAIL_CAMPAIGN_2020_01_29_04_11&utm_medium=email&utm_term=0_c459f924d0-134ccc685e-61144595
13 Brook, Dr Orian. O'Brien, Dr David. Taylor, Dr Mark. "Panic! Survey into Social Class, Taste and Inequalities", https://createlondon.org/wp-content/uploads/2018/04/Panic-Social-Class-Taste-and-Inequalities-in-the-Creative-Industries1.pdf 2018 - p13
14 Brook, Dr Orian. O'Brien, Dr David. Taylor, Dr Mark. Op. Cit. – p7
15 Brook, Dr Orian. O'Brien, Dr David. Taylor, Dr Mark. Op. Cit. – p14-15
16 Brook, Dr Orian. O'Brien, Dr David. Taylor, Dr Mark. Op. Cit. – p11
17 Brook, Dr Orian. O'Brien, Dr David. Taylor, Dr Mark. Op. Cit. – p2
18 Brook, Dr Orian. O'Brien, Dr David. Taylor, Dr Mark. Op. Cit. – p4
19 Brook, Dr Orian. O'Brien, Dr David. Taylor, Dr Mark. Op. Cit. – p4
20 Brook, Dr Orian. O'Brien, Dr David. Taylor, Dr Mark. Op. Cit. – p33
21 Brook, Dr Orian. O'Brien, Dr David. Taylor, Dr Mark. Op. Cit. – p20
22 Brook, Dr Orian. O'Brien, Dr David. Taylor, Dr Mark. Op. Cit. – p24
23 Jerry Saltz on the Contemporary Art World: The Good, The Bad and The Very Bad, https://www.youtube.com/watch?v=VGmaXK3-7Bc 2018
24 Tim Marlow: Favourite Projects / Advice for Selling Work https://www.youtube.com/watch?v=c8oOP3f6qkl 2014
25 https://quoteinvestigator.com/2013/03/06/artists-steal/
26 Resch, Dr Magnus. Become an Art Market Insider - How the Art Industry Really Works - #TOA18 https://www.youtube.com/watch?v=E2JfJBmGa7s 2018
27 Padgett, Anthony "How To Find And Create An Original Art Masterpiece" 2018 ADP Publishing
28 Elgammal, Ahmed. Mazzone, Marian. Liu, Bingchen. Kim, Diana. Elhoseiny, Mohamed. "The Shape of Art History in the eyes of the Machine" from 32nd AAAI conference on Artificial Intelligence, New Orleans, USA 2018
29 https://www.telegraph.co.uk/science/2020/01/30/rachmaninoff-innovative-composer-eversays-computer/
30 https://mindmatters.ai/2019/06/ai-can-detect-art-forgery-and-thats-not-all/
31 Elgammal, Ahmed. Liu, Bingchen. Elhoseiny, Mohamed. Mazzone, Marian. "CAN: Creative Adversarial Networks Generating "Art" by Learning About Styles and Deviating from Style Norms" from 8th International Conference on Computational Creativity (ICCC), Atlanta, GA, 2017 p19-20
32 Elgammal, Ahmed. Liu, Bingchen. Elhoseiny, Mohamed. Mazzone, Marian. Op. Cit. p21
33 https://aiartists.org/unanswered-questions
34 Cogswell, David and Butzer, C.M. Op. Cit. p160

BIBLIOGRAPHY

Birch, Lionel "The History of the T.U.C. 1868 – 1968" The General Council of the Trades Union Congress, 1968

Brook, Dr Orian. O'Brien, Dr David. Taylor, Dr Mark "Panic Social Class Taste and Inequalities in the Creative Industries"

Cogswell, David and Butzer, C.M. "Unions For Beginners" 2012, For Beginners LLC

Elgammal, Ahmed. Liu, Bingchen. Elhoseiny, Mohamed. Mazzone, Marian. "CAN: Creative Adversarial Networks Generating "Art" by Learning About Styles and Deviating from Style Norms" from 8th International Conference on Computational Creativity (ICCC), Atlanta, GA, 2017

Elgammal, Ahmed. Mazzone, Marian. Liu, Bingchen. Kim, Diana. Elhoseiny, Mohamed. "The Shape of Art History in the eyes of the Machine" from 32nd AAAI conference on Artificial Intelligence, New Orleans, USA 2018

Padgett, Anthony "How To Find And Create An Original Art Masterpiece" 2018 ADP Publishing

Savage, Katharine "The Story of British Trade Unions", Kestrel Books 1977

Brook, Dr Orian. O'Brien, Dr David. Taylor, Dr Mark. https://createlondon.org/wp-content/uploads/2018/04/Panic-Social-Class-Taste-and-Inequalities-in-the-Creative-Industries1.pdf 2018